D0602348

*Origami*

Book Two

Japanese Paper-Folding

by
**Florence Sakade**

CHARLES E. TUTTLE COMPANY

tland, Vermont          Tokyo, Japan

*Published by the Charles E. Tuttle Company, Inc.*
*of Rutland, Vermont & Tokyo, Japan*
*with editorial offices at*
*Suido 1-chome, 2-6, Bunkyo-ku, Tokyo, Japan*

*©1958 by Charles E. Tuttle Co., Inc.*

*Library of Congress Catalog Card No. 57-10685*

*International Standard Book No. 0-8048-0455-9*

*First edition, 1958*
*Sixth-second printing, 1998*

PRINTED IN SINGAPORE

# Table of Contents

# Introduction

It is amazing how a Japanese child can create intricate figures through step-by-step foldings of square pieces of colored paper. This favorite hobby of paper-folding, or *origami,* is an art that in Japan has a tradition of centuries and still occupies an important place in the life of every child.

Those already familiar with my first book of *origami* will find the figures introduced in this second book easy to fold. Here, again, I have avoided figures too complicated and have limited myself to the presentation of simpler ones, the kind that can be folded even by the beginner after a little practice. Those who have tried their skill at the first book will find that some of the foldings in this are already familiar. I have referred to the pages in the first book on which fuller explanation of some of the foldings can be found, but I also believe that the directions in this book are sufficient in themselves.

Some objects here included are completed by drawing and the use of scissors to produce a more recognizable effect. It is essential that the colored paper to be used be always perfectly square. On page 32 of this book I have introduced the use of *origami* creations in a finger-play. A wider use for and greater three-dimensional effect of *origami* figures can be acquired on sand tables and murals in classrooms.

While the child enjoys *origami* as a fascinating pastime, parents and teachers can see that Japanese paper-folding has definite educational effect: *ability to follow directions* is an invaluable advantage throughout school life and thereafter, and here the child is faced with the fact that he will not get results by doing just what he wants. The step-by-step following of directions such as are in this book inevitably results in an increase of *patience*. There must be accuracy and *concentrated attention*—for proper shapes can be obtained only through careful, symmetrical foldings—the practice of which will in time help remedy carelessness and inattention. The child must select from among papers of different colors that which most suits the subject, which will awaken a consciousness of *harmony* and encourage greater *observation* of the world about him.

Japanese paper-folding, then, offers not only hours of peaceful recreation and that indescribable pleasure of accomplishment when a solid figure has been made from a little piece of paper, but forms the mind and gives control and skill to the fingers of those who enjoy it.

I owe my gratitude to Mr. Kazuhiko Sono for his invaluable assistance in the preparation of this book and also to Mr. T. Morikuni for collaborating on the diagrams.

FLORENCE SAKADE

# Wolf

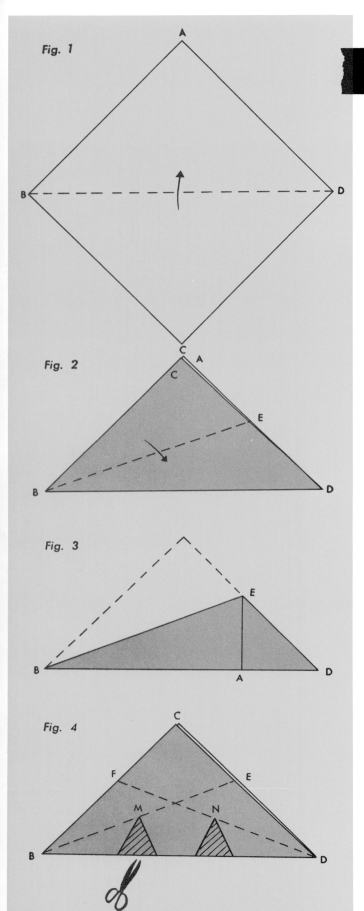

Fig. 1

Fig. 2

Fig. 3

Fig. 4

1.   Fold a square piece of paper along line BD (Fig. 1) so that corner C falls on corner A (Fig. 2).

2.   Crease BE by bringing BC and BA down to fall on BD (Figs. 2 & 3).

3.   Make another crease as in step 2 along FD. Then cut out two triangles at M and N (Fig. 4).

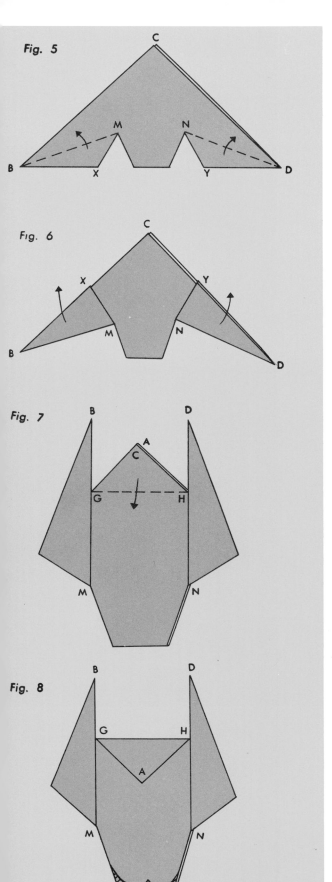

Fig. 5

Fig. 6

Fig. 7

Fig. 8

4. Fold along BM and DN (Fig. 5) so that X and Y fall on BC and DC respectively (Fig. 6).

5. Fold corners B and D upward (Fig. 6) so that BM and DN are about vertical (Fig. 7).

6. Fold along GH (Fig. 7), bringing corners C and A forward (Fig. 8).

7. Turn the paper over, draw the face, and cut out the mouth.

# Dog

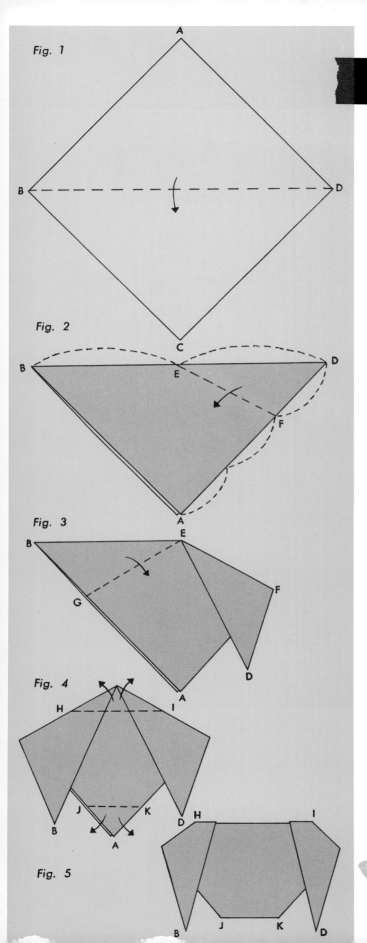

Fig. 1

Fig. 2

Fig. 3

Fig. 4

Fig. 5

1.  Fold a square piece of paper along line BD (Fig. 1) so that corner A falls on corner C (Fig. 2).

2.  Fold along EF (Fig. 2), bringing corner D forward (Fig. 3). Point F is one-third of the way down DA (Fig. 2).

3.  Repeat step 2 on the other side at EG (Figs. 3 & 4).

4.  Fold back along HI and JK (Fig. 4), and then draw the face.

# Cat

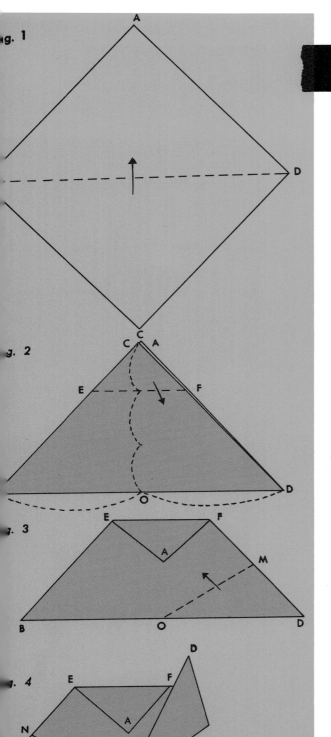

Fig. 1

Fig. 2

Fig. 3

Fig. 4

Fig. 5

1.   Fold a square piece of paper along line BD (Fig. 1) so that corner C falls on corner A (Fig. 2).

2.   Fold along EF (Fig. 2), bringing corners C and A forward (Fig. 3). EF is about one-third of the way down CO (Fig. 2).

3.   Fold along OM (Fig. 3), bringing corner D up so that OD meets F (Fig. 4).

4.   Repeat step 3 on the other side at ON (Figs. 4 & 5).

5.   Turn the paper over and draw the face.

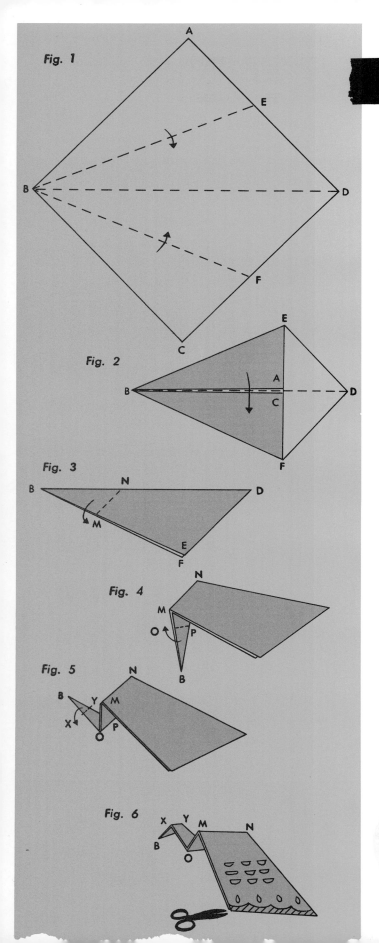

# Peacock

1.   Fold a square piece of paper along lines BE and BF (Fig. 1) so that edges BA and BC meet at the center BD (Fig. 2).

2.   Fold along BD (Fig. 2) so that E falls on F (Fig. 3).

3.   Fold back point B along MN (Figs. 3 & 4).

4.   Fold along OP, bringing point B back and upward (Figs. 4 & 5).

5.   Make the head by folding along XY, turning point B back and downward to the left (Fig. 5).

6.   Draw the feathers and cut their ends (Fig. 6).

Note:   By using two papers of different colors, one placed on top of the other, the feathers can be cut out from the top paper and the other color will show from the inside.

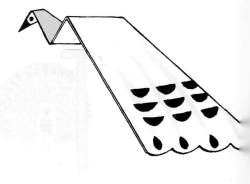

# Peahen

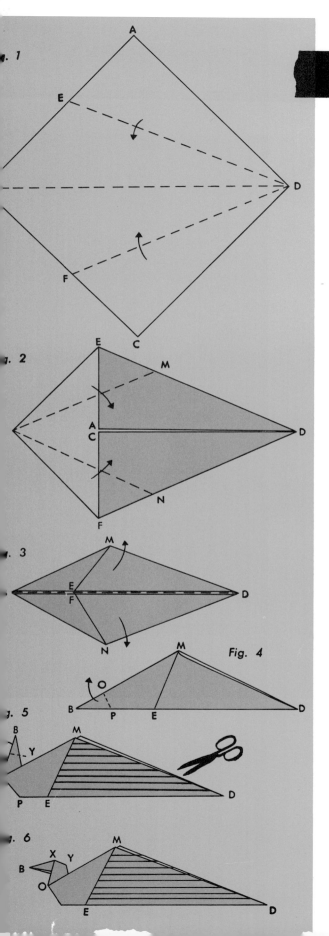

1. Fold a square piece of paper along lines DE and DF (Fig. 1) so that edges AD and CD meet at the center BD (Fig. 2).

2. Fold along BM and BN (Fig. 2) so that BE and BF meet at BD (Fig. 3).

3. Fold in half outward along BD (Figs. 3 & 4).

4. Fold back point B along OP (Figs. 4 & 5).

5. Make the head by folding along XY, turning point B back and downward to the left (Figs. 5 & 6).

6. Cut lines parallel to ED to make the feathers (Figs. 5 & 6).

# Giraffe

**Fig. 1**

**Fig. 2**

**Fig. 3**

**Fig. 4**

**Fig. 5**

**Fig. 6**

**Fig. 7**

**Fig. 8**

1.  Fold a square piece of paper along lines AE and AF (Fig. 1) so that edges AB and AD meet at the center AC (Fig. 2).

2.  Fold in half at AC (Fig. 2) so that AE falls on AF (Fig. 3).

3.  Fold along OM and ON, inserting point M between the two body flaps. O is a little less than halfway down AE. (Figs. 3 & 4).

4.  Fold in along AE (Fig. 5) so that point O is inside the body flap.

5.  Turn the paper over and repeat step 4 on the other side (Fig. 6).

6.  Cut out the legs (Fig. 7), make slit XY on the back of the neck to make the head and ears (Figs. 7 & 8), cut off A (Fig. 8), and draw the eyes.

# Clown

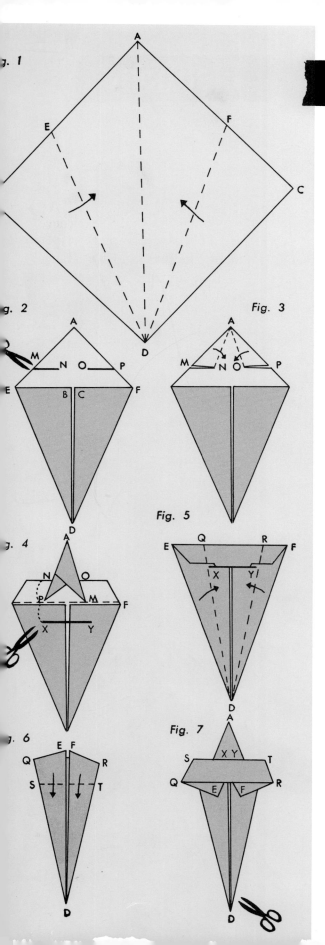

*g. 1*

*g. 2*  Fig. 3

Fig. 5

*g. 4*

*g. 6*  Fig. 7

1. Fold a square piece of paper along lines DE and DF (Fig. 1) so that edges BD and CD meet at the center AD (Fig. 2).

2. Cut MN and PO (Fig. 2).

3. Fold along AN and AO (Fig. 3) so that the two side flaps overlap each other (Fig. 4).

4. Cut XY about the length of NO and no more than half an inch below EF (Fig. 4).

5. Fold along EF (Fig. 4), bringing point A forward and through slit XY (Fig. 5).

6. Fold along QD and RD (Fig. 5) so that points E and F meet at center (Fig. 6).

7. Fold along ST (Fig. 6), bringing QR forward, and point A will come up by itself (Fig. 7). Line ST is on XY.

8. To make the legs, cut the lower part of AD from D (Fig. 7).

9. Turn the paper over and draw the face.

# Elephant

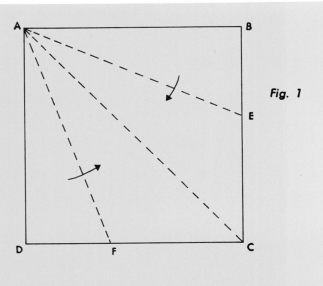

Fig. 1

1. Fold a square piece of paper along lines AE and AF (Fig. 1) so that AB and AD meet at the center AC (Fig. 2).

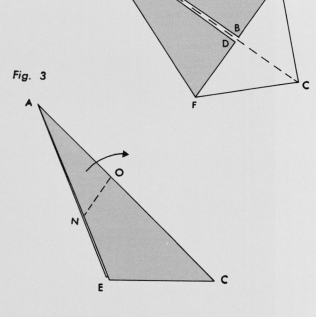

Fig. 2

Fig. 3

2. Fold along AC (Fig. 2) so that corner E falls on corner F (Fig. 3).

3. Fold along ON (Fig. 3), bringing point A forward and across to the right so that NA is about parallel to EC (Fig. 4).

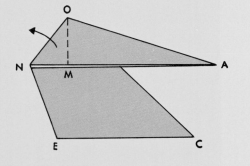

Fig. 4

4. Lift the top flap at M (Fig. 4) and open corner O,

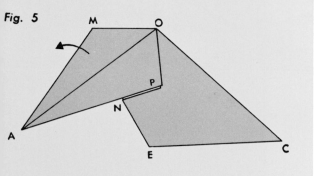

Fig. 5

bringing point A across to the left so that OA falls almost on ON (Fig. 5).

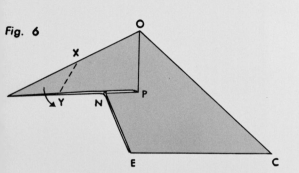

Fig. 6

5.  Fold back point M along OA (Figs. 5 & 6).

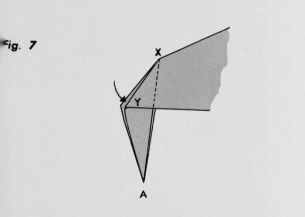

Fig. 7

6.  Crease XY (Fig. 6), separate the two flaps of the ears, and bring point A down between the flaps (Fig. 7).

7.  Draw the eyes and cut out the legs and tail (Fig. 8).

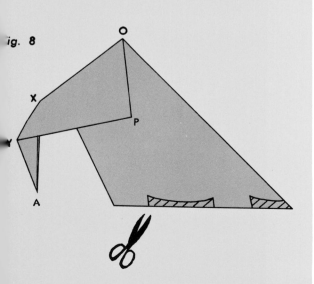

Fig. 8

# Kimono

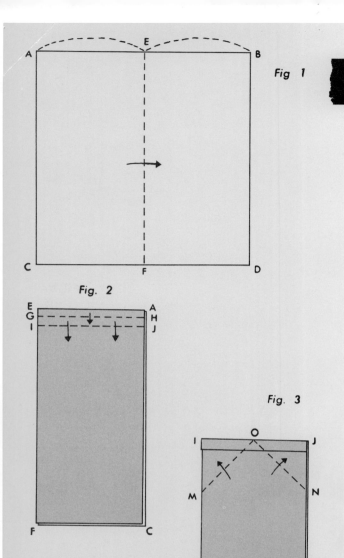

Fig 1

Fig. 2

Fig. 3

Fig. 4

1. Fold a square sheet of paper along line EF (Fig. 1) so that AC falls on BD (Fig. 2).

2. Fold forward at GH, about one-quarter of an inch down from EA, and once more at IJ (Figs. 2 & 3).

3. Fold back corners I and J along OM and ON (Fig. 3) so that OI and OJ meet at the center in the back (Fig. 4). Point O is halfway between I and J.

4. Fold back point O along PQ, and then fold forward along RS so that PQ falls on FD (Figs. 4 & 5).

Fig. 5

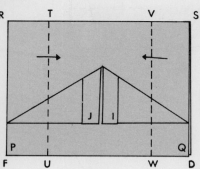

Fig. 6

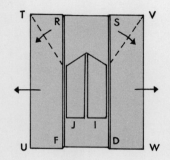

Fig. 7

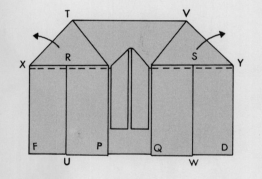

Fig. 8

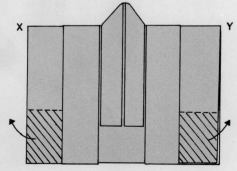

5. Fold along TU and VW (Fig. 5) so that RF and SD touch the collar lines J and I respectively (Fig. 6).

6. Lift F, separating it from P, and open corner R so that point R falls on TU. Do the same with D and S. (Figs. 6 & 7).

7. Fold back along XY (Figs. 7 & 8).

8. To make the sleeves, fold back only the back flap (Fig. 8).

Note: An oblong piece of paper or cloth about three times as long as it is wide can be used as well to make this kimono. In that case, step 1 would be omitted.

# Rabbit

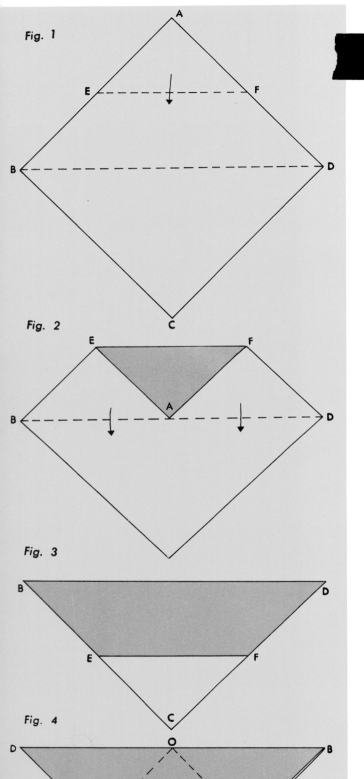

**Fig. 1**

**Fig. 2**

**Fig. 3**

**Fig. 4**

1. Fold a square piece of paper along line EF (Fig. 1) so that corner A touches BD at the center (Fig. 2).

2. Fold forward along BD (Figs. 2 & 3).

3. Turn the paper over and fold along OG and OH (Fig. 4), bringing corners D and B forward to meet at C (Fig. 5).

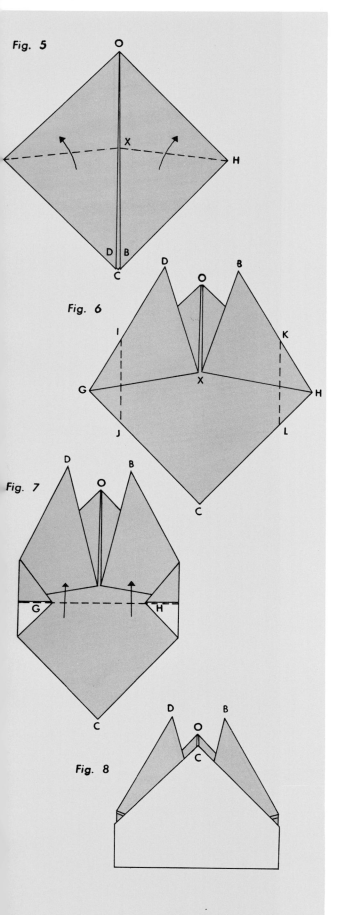

Fig. 5

Fig. 6

Fig. 7

Fig. 8

4. Fold along xG and xH (Fig. 5), bringing corners D and B up, but off o (Fig. 6). Point x then is not on GH but a little higher up on co.

5. Fold along IJ and KL (Fig. 6) so that points G and H come forward on GH (Fig. 7).

6. Fold along GH (Fig. 7) so that corner C falls on o (Fig. 8).

7. Turn the paper over and draw the face and ears.

Note: Use this rabbit for the goats in the finger-play on page 32.

# Fox

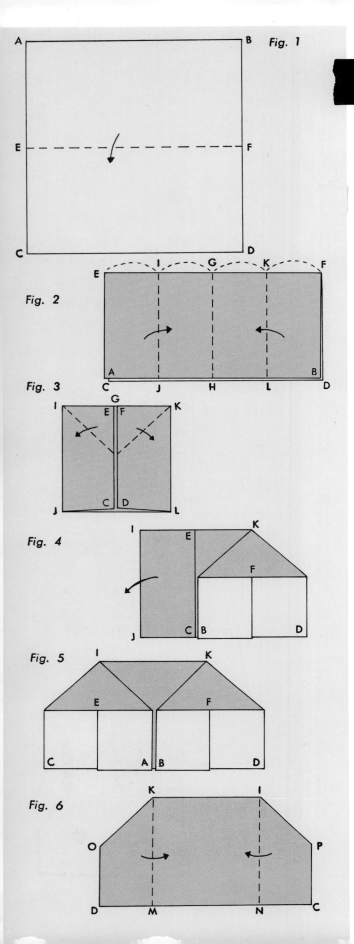

Fig. 1

Fig. 2

Fig. 3

Fig. 4

Fig. 5

Fig. 6

1. Fold a square piece of paper along line EF (Fig. 1) so that AB falls on CD (Fig. 2).

2. Fold along IJ and KL (Fig. 2) so that edges AEC and BDF meet at center GH (Fig. 3).

3. Open corner F (Fig. 3) by lifting D toward the right while holding B in place (Fig. 4).

4. Repeat step 3 with ECA (Figs. 4 & 5), (See *Origami: Book I,* p. 17, "House," Figs. 1–5) and turn the paper over (Fig. 6).

5. Fold along KM and IN (Fig. 6) so that edges OD and PC meet at the center (Fig. 7).

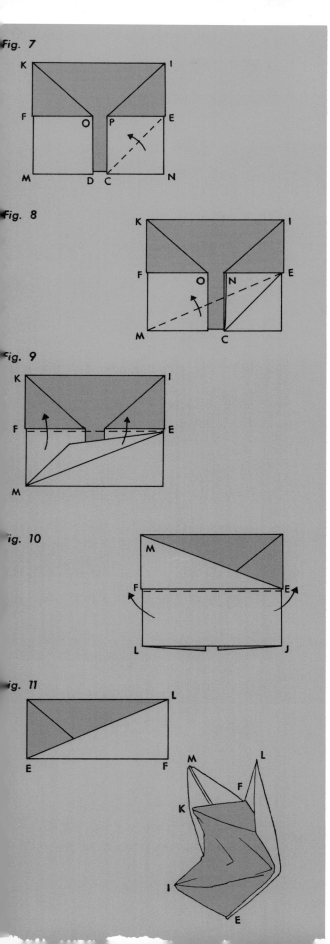

Fig. 7

Fig. 8

Fig. 9

Fig. 10

Fig. 11

6. Fold the top flap along EC (Fig. 7) so that N falls on P (Fig. 8).

7. Fold along EM (Figs. 8 & 9).

8. Fold the top flap along FE (Fig. 9) so that point M falls on K (Fig. 10).

9. Turn the paper over and repeat steps 7, 8, and 9, but note that L is on the right-hand side while M was on the left (Fig. 11).

10. Separate the two flaps by putting your thumb into I and index finger into K from the back under EF (Fig. 11). Push back the middle part of the face with the other hand, and the ears, L and M, will stand up (Fig. 12). Move the two fingers so that K and I meet.

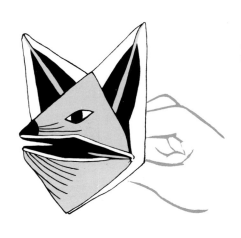

# Robin

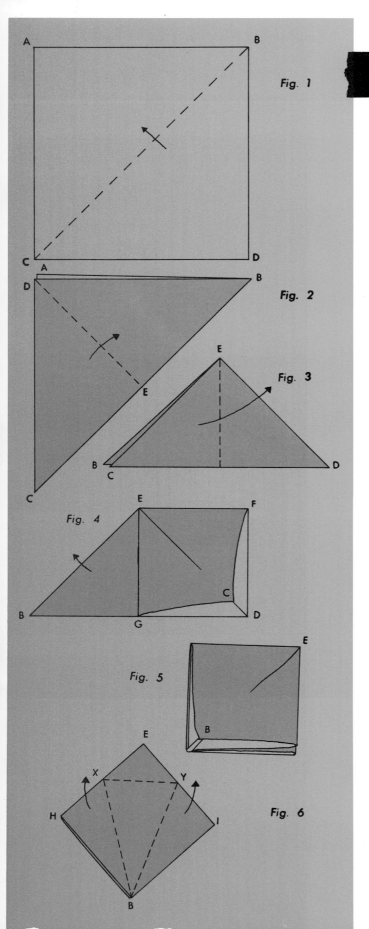

Fig. 1

Fig. 2

Fig. 3

Fig. 4

Fig. 5

Fig. 6

1. Fold a square piece of paper along line BC (Fig. 1) so that corner D falls on corner A (Fig. 2).

2. Fold along ED (Fig. 2) so that point C falls on B (Fig. 3).

3. Open C (Fig. 3) and bring it over to the right, directly above D (Fig. 4). Place C on D and crease EF and EG (Fig. 4).

4. Turn the paper over and repeat step 3 with B (Figs. 4 & 5).

5. Crease at XB and YB (Fig. 6) so that HB and IB meet at EB.

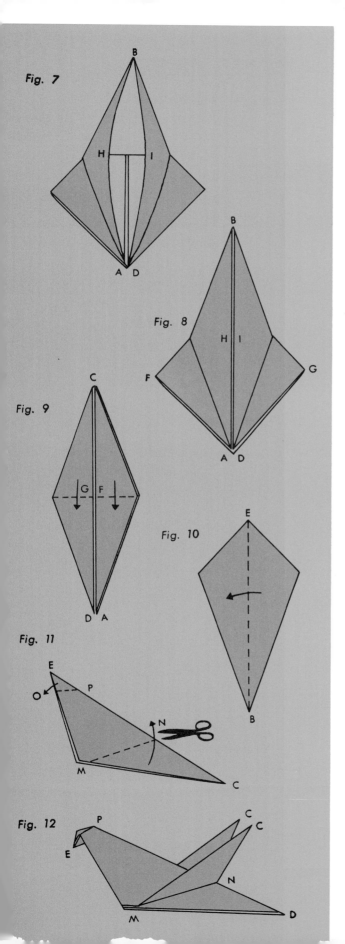

Fig. 7

Fig. 8

Fig. 9

Fig. 10

Fig. 11

Fig. 12

6. Lift up B and fold at XY (Fig. 6) so that H and I meet at the middle on BA and BD respectively (Figs. 7 & 8).

7. Turn the paper over and repeat steps 5 and 6 (Fig. 9). (See *Origami: Book I,* pp. 30–31, "Crane," Figs. 1–10.)

8. Bring point C down on AD (Fig. 9), and do the same with B on the reverse side (Fig. 10).

9. Fold in half along EB (Figs. 10 & 11). Then cut the top flap along CN, N being halfway up CE (Fig. 11).

10. Lift up C and fold along MN (Fig. 11) so that MN is about perpendicular to ME (Fig. 12).

11. Turn the paper over and repeat step 10 on the other side.

12. Crease at OP (Fig. 11), separate the two body flaps, and bring point E down between the flaps (Fig. 12). (See Fig. 7 in "Elephant," p. 15.)

# Clock

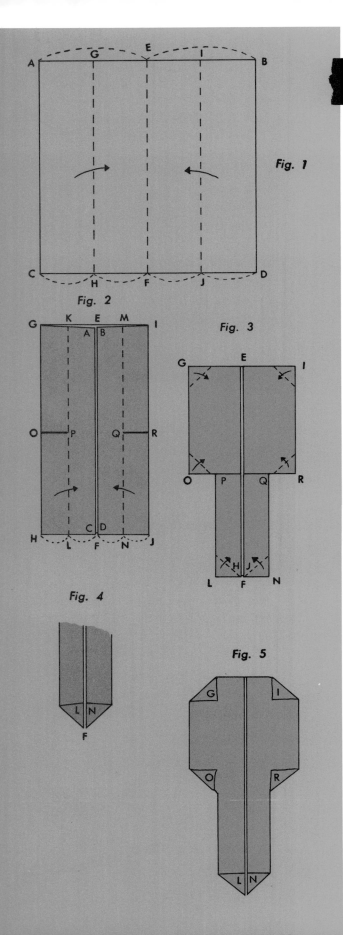

**Fig. 1**

**Fig. 2**

**Fig. 3**

**Fig. 4**

**Fig. 5**

1. Fold a square piece of paper along lines GH and IJ (Fig. 1) so that edges AC and BD meet at the center EF (Fig. 2).

2. Cut at OP and RQ, making GIRO an approximate square (Fig. 2).

3. Fold along PL and QN (Fig. 2) so that OH and RJ meet at EF (Fig. 3).

4. Fold corners G, I, R, and O forward (Figs. 3 & 5).

5. Fold corners L and N (Figs. 3 & 4) forward so that they meet on EF (Fig. 4).

6. Turn the paper over and draw the face and pendulum.

# Rowboat

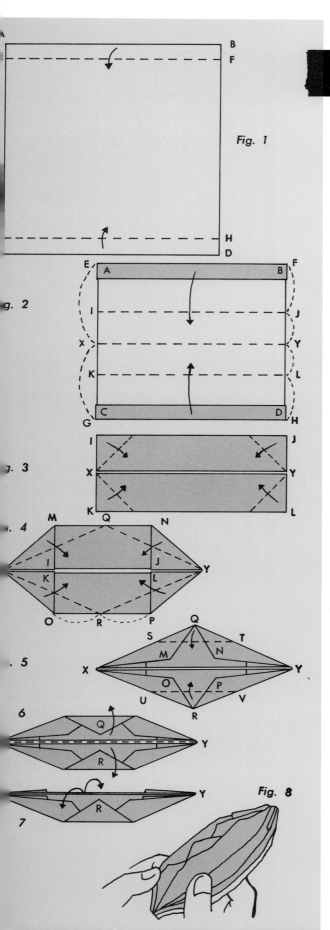

Fig. 1

Fig. 2

Fig. 3

Fig. 4

Fig. 5

Fig. 6

Fig. 7

Fig. 8

1. Fold in opposite ends of a square piece of paper about one-quarter of an inch from each edge along lines EF and GH (Figs. 1 & 2).

2. Fold along IJ and KL (Fig. 2) so that EF and GH meet at the center XY (Fig. 3).

3. Fold corners I, J, K, and L (Fig. 3) forward so that XI, YJ, XK, and YL fall on XY (Fig. 4).

4. Fold along XQ, QY, XR and RY (Fig. 4), bringing corners M, N, O, and P forward (Fig. 5). Point Q and R are the centers of MN and OP respectively.

5. Fold along ST and UV (Fig. 5), bringing corners O and R forward (Fig. 6).

6. Fold out in half along XY (Figs. 6 & 7).

7. Take the two outer flaps (Fig. 7), one in each hand, and turn the entire object inside out (Fig. 8).

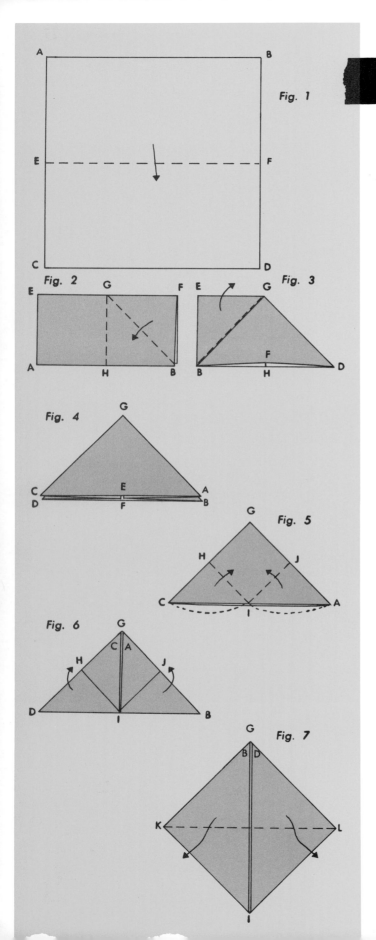

Fig. 1

Fig. 2

Fig. 3

Fig. 4

Fig. 5

Fig. 6

Fig. 7

# Church

1. Fold a square piece of paper along line EF (Fig. 1) so that AB falls on CD (Fig. 2).

2. Crease in the middle at GH (Fig. 2).

3. Open corner F (Fig. 2) and bring point F down between B and D so that GF falls on GH Fig. 3). Crease GB and GD.

4. Turn the paper over and repeat step 3 with E (Fig. 4). (See *Origami: Book I,* p. 14, "Flowers," Figs. 1–4.)

5. Fold along HI and JI (Fig. 5) so that points C and A meet at G (Fig. 6).

6. Turn the paper over and repeat step 5 with B and D (Fig. 7).

7. Open corner B (Fig. 7) and bring point B down so that KB falls on KI (Fig. 8)

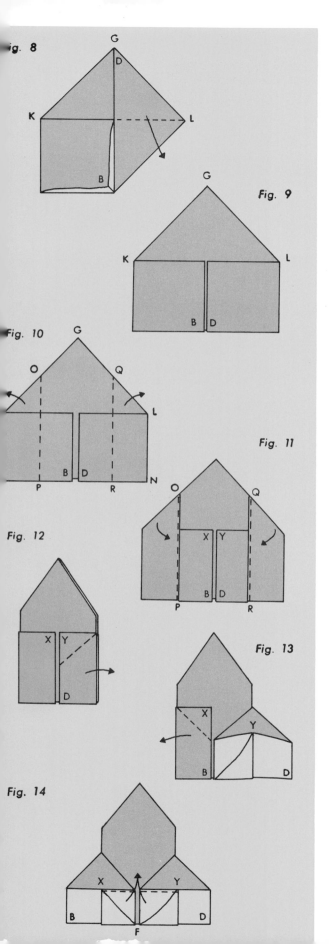

Fig. 8

Fig. 9

Fig. 10

Fig. 11

Fig. 12

Fig. 13

Fig. 14

8. Repeat step 7 with corner D (Figs. 8 & 9).

9. Turn the paper over and repeat steps 7 and 8.

10. Fold back along OP and QR (Fig. 10) so that KM will be under flap OP and LN under flap QR (Fig. 11).

11. Turn the paper over and repeat step 10 on the other side (Fig. 12).

12. Open corner Y (Figs. 12 & 13).

13. Open corner X (Figs. 13 & 14).

14. Fold along XY (Fig. 14), bringing point F up.

15. Turn the paper over and repeat steps 12, 13, and 14.

16. Draw the cross, windows, and doors.

Note: Use this church for the house in the finger-play on page 32.

# Flower

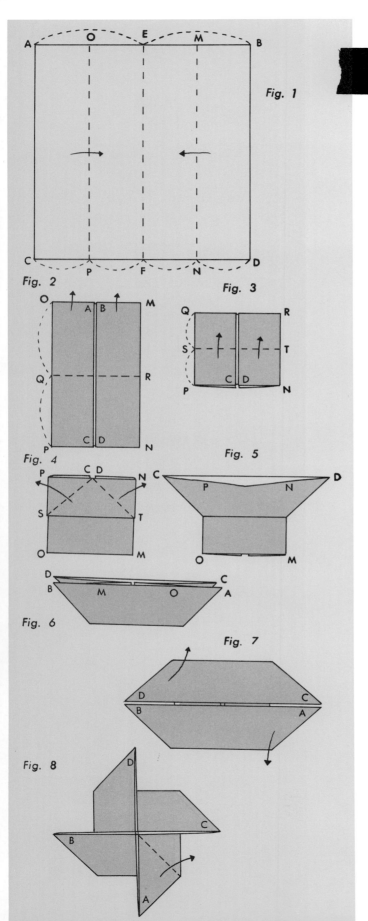

Fig. 1

Fig. 2

Fig. 3

Fig. 4

Fig. 5

Fig. 6

Fig. 7

Fig. 8

1. Fold a square piece of paper along lines OP and MN (Fig. 1) so that edges AC and BD meet at the center EF (Fig. 2).

2. Fold OM back along QR (Fig. 2) so that OM will be under PN (Fig. 3).

3. Fold along ST (Fig. 3) so that PN falls on QR (Fig. 4).

4. Make a crease along CS and DT (Fig. 4) and then pull out corners C and D (Fig. 5).

5. Turn the paper over and repeat steps 3 and 4 (Fig. 6).

6. Spread out Fig. 6 so that it looks like Fig. 7.

7. Fold D upward and A downward (Figs. 7 & 8). (See *Origami: Book I,* p. 26, "Windmill," Figs. 1–9.)

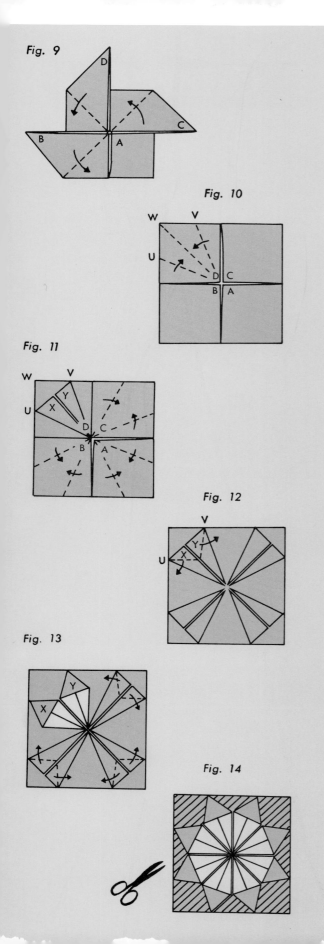

Fig. 9

Fig. 10

Fig. 11

Fig. 12

Fig. 13

Fig. 14

8. Open corner A (Fig. 8) and bring point A to the center (Fig. 9).

9. Repeat step 8 at B, C, and D (Figs. 9 & 10).

10. Fold along UD and VD (Fig. 10) so that XD and YD meet at the center WD (Fig. 11).

11. Repeat step 10 on the other three squares (Figs. 11 & 12).

12. Open corners X and Y (Fig. 12) and fold them flat (Fig. 13).

13. Repeat step 12 with the other six corners (Fig. 13 & 14).

14. Cut off those portions shaded in Fig. 14.

# Candy Box

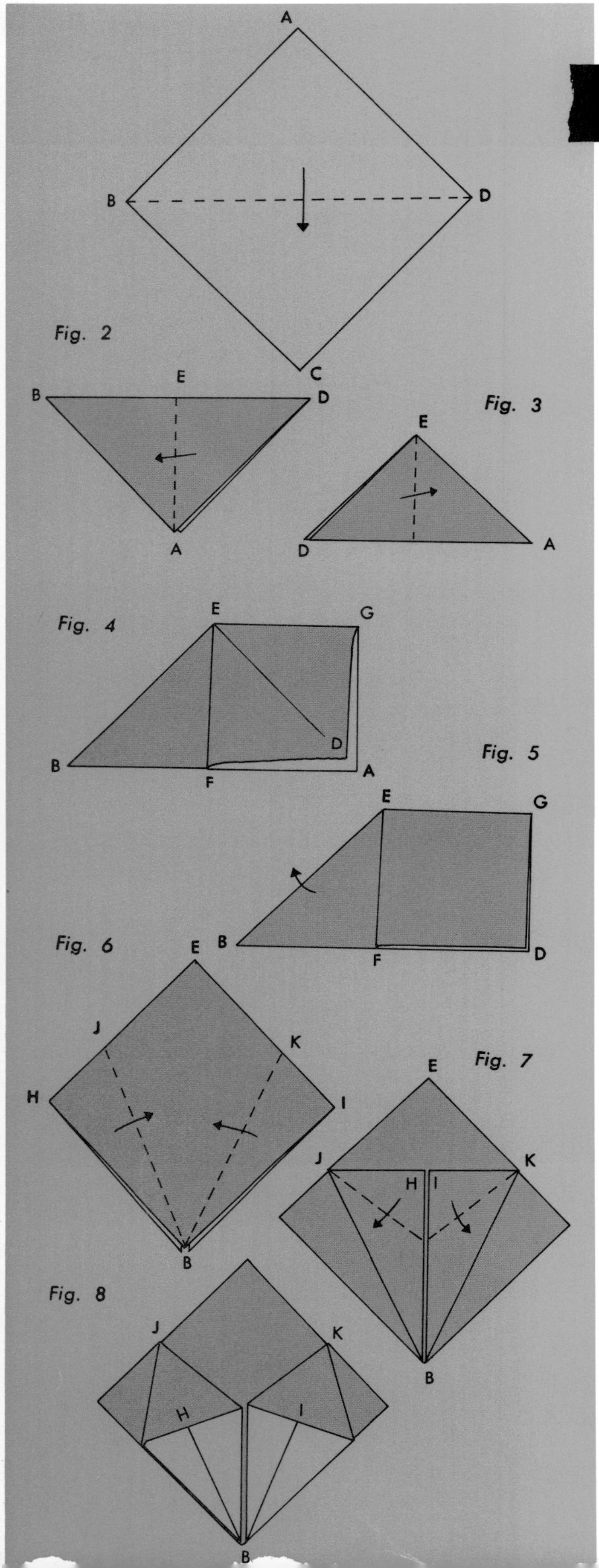

Fig. 2

Fig. 3

Fig. 4

Fig. 5

Fig. 6

Fig. 7

Fig. 8

1. Fold a square piece of paper along line BD (Fig. 1) so that corner A falls on corner C (Fig. 2).

2. Fold along EA (Fig. 2) so that corner D falls on B (Fig. 3).

3. Open corner D (Fig. 3) and bring it over to the right until it is directly above A (Fig. 4). Then crease along EF and EG (Fig. 5).

4. Turn the paper over and repeat step 3 with B (Fig. 6).

5. Fold along BJ and BK (Fig. 6) so that BH and BI meet at BE (Fig. 7). (See *Origami: Book I,* p. 30, "Crane," Figs. 1–6).

6. Open corner H and I (Fig. 7) so that JH falls on JB and KI on KB (Fig. 8).

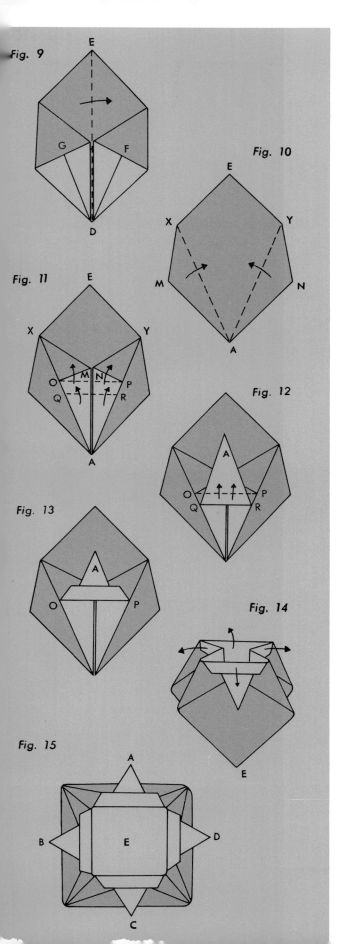

Fig. 9

Fig. 10

Fig. 11

Fig. 12

Fig. 13

Fig. 14

Fig. 15

7. Turn the paper over and repeat steps 5 and 6 (Fig. 9).

8. Fold only the top flap along ED (Fig. 9), and bring G on top of F. Then turn the paper over and bring I on top of H (Fig. 10).

9. Fold along XA and YA (Fig. 10) so that MA and NA meet at EA (Fig. 11).

10. Fold along QR (Fig. 11), bringing A forward and up (Fig. 12).

11. Fold along OP (Figs. 12 & 13).

12. Turn the paper over and repeat steps 9, 10, and 11 on the other side with corner C, and then with B and D (Fig. 14).

13. Carefully insert your fingers into the object and flatten E (Fig. 15).

# Origami Finger-Play

Do you see the big bad wolf creeping up from behind the tree, and the seven little frightened goats? You will notice that most of the figures that you find in this picture are made from *origami* which you have thus far learned in this book: flowers, birds, giraffe, wolf, building (from "Church"), goats (from "Rabbit," the ends of the ears folded outward), and trees (from *Origami: Book I*). Objects made from *origami* can be arranged in this manner and used as backgrounds for plays. It will be interesting to combine various figures made from square pieces of different-sized papers and create your own sceneries for some of your stories.